MW00745397

Tender Flower and the Medicine

A Native American Folktale

by Adam Coleman

NATIONAL
GEOGRAPHIC
LEARNING

CENGAGE
Learning

Long ago, there was a girl named
Tender Flower. She lived in a village next
to a big forest. Every day she walked with
her dog, Tic, into the forest.

"I know this forest so well," she said.
"I can walk through it with my eyes closed."

In the winter, snow fell over Tender Flower's village. Snow covered the forest trails, but Tender Flower still walked in the forest every day.

One morning, Tender Flower heard the sounds of coughs and sneezes coming from inside the village homes.

Tender Flower's father looked worried.

"Many of our people are sick," he said. "They have fevers with headaches and stomachaches. This is a very bad sickness."

Soon, everyone in the village was sick, even Tender Flower's family. Only Tender Flower remained healthy.

Tender Flower's father called to her from his bed.

"We need medicine," he said. "Go to the village on the other side of the forest. Ask the people of the village for help. I can not go myself. I am too sick."

Tender Flower called to Tic, and they ran into the forest together.

They ran through the snow like forest animals. They ran so hard and fast, they didn't even feel cold. Although she was very tired, Tender Flower told herself to keep running.

Soon, Tender Flower arrived at the other village. She told the chief about the sickness in her village. "Take this medicine," said the chief. "It will help your people. If they are weak, give it to them yourself." "Thank you, great chief," said Tender Flower.

Tender Flower put the medicine bag around her neck. She did not stop to eat or to drink. She and Tic ran back into the forest toward her village. They ran even faster than before.

Now, the snow fell harder. It was night. A strong wind blew into Tender Flower's face. The cold made her feet ache. Soon, she was dizzy from running.

Tender Flower didn't think about herself. She thought only about the sick people in her village.

When Tender Flower was near her village, she fell. Her slippers got stuck in the deep snow and came off her feet. Still she kept running. Her feet were covered with cuts, but she kept going.

Finally, she reached home and gave the medicine to the sick people in her village.

Soon, the medicine made everyone better.

In the spring, Tender Flower went to the place where she lost her slippers. The slippers were not there. Instead, in their place, there were beautiful flowers.

The people now call these flowers "Lady's Slippers." The flowers remind everyone of the brave girl, Tender Flower, and of how she saved her people.

Facts About Medicines

For thousands of years, people have used plants as medicines. Long ago, people learned that some plants helped heal cuts and bruises. Other plants helped people recover from colds and fevers. Today, plants are still used to make many medicines.

Quinine is a medicine that comes from a rain forest plant. It protects people from a sickness called malaria. Before quinine, malaria killed many people around the world.

Many of the plants that people use for medicines today come from Earth's rain forests. Rain forests are home to more than half of all types of plants on Earth. Scientists say that rain forest plants probably hold the key to many more important medicines.

But rain forests around the world are in danger. People are cutting down many rain forests. When this happens, important plants are lost forever. Without these plants, important medicines can not be discovered. This is one important reason to protect Earth's rain forests.

Rain forests are disappearing because people are cutting them down. People cut down rain forests to get the wood from the trees, to clear the land for farms, and to build roads.

Fun with Health

What problem does each person have?
Write a sentence with one of the words.

cough	bruise	cut	headache	stomachache	fever

1. <u>He has a</u>
   <u>fever.</u>

2. _____
   _____

3. _____
   _____

4. _____
   _____

5. _____
   _____

6. _____
   _____

Put each word in the correct place in the puzzle.

headache   fever   sneeze   medicine

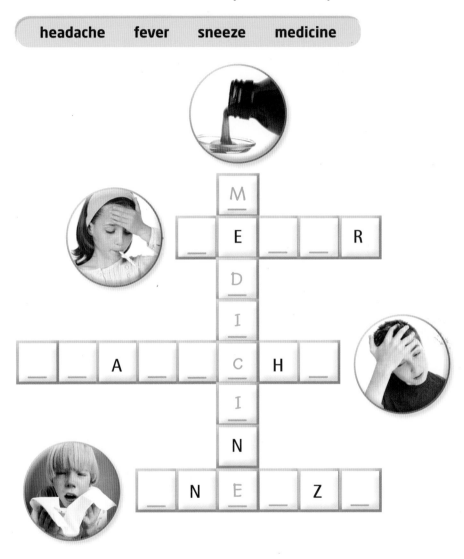

When were you last sick? How did you get better? Write three sentences about it. Use a bilingual dictionary if necessary.

Glossary

chief the leader of a group of people

heal to make a sickness better

remind to tell people about something so that people remember it

sickness being sick or not well

slippers

slippers soft shoes

tender soft, gentle

trails a path through a forest that people walk on

trails

village a small town of just a few houses

village

weak not strong, sick